HOW TO DEAL WITH FEARFUL AVOIDANT ATTACHMENT STYLE

Breaking Free from Emotional Barriers: A Comprehensive Guide to Understanding, Overcoming, and Thriving with Fearful-Avoidant Attachment

NELLIE HUGHES

Copyright©2023 Nellie Hughes

All Rights Reserved

INTRODUCTION

CHAPTER ONE

What Is Exactly Fearful Avoidant Attachment
Signs of fearful avoidant attachment
The Signs in children
The Signs in adults

CHAPTER TWO

What led to the causes fearful avoidant attachment?
Is it possible for a fearful-avoidant attachment style to undergo changes as time progresses?

CHAPTER THREE

The Impact of Fearful-Avoidant Attachment Style on Your Life
How to Overcome Fearful Avoidant Attachment style

CONCLUSION

INTRODUCTION

People acquire the ability to form connections with others through their interactions with their parents.

Infants whose needs are fulfilled are prone to cultivating secure and emotionally resilient personalities, while those whose needs are unmet may exhibit anxious, avoidant, or even fearful traits.

The personality you cultivate can greatly influence various aspects of your life, particularly impacting how you establish and sustain relationships.

Individuals with a fearful avoidant attachment style often crave closeness and intimacy in their relationships. Despite this desire, they may struggle to attain the profound connection they yearn for.

This is due to their past attachment experiences instilling a fear of intimacy in them. In certain instances, their personality may incline them to actively avoid forming close connections. This pattern can result in tumultuous relationships marked by intense emotional fluctuations.

Comprehending the characteristics of fearful avoidant attachment can provide insight into your relationship behaviors. If you suspect a loved one possesses this attachment style, recognizing the origins of their instincts may assist you in responding to them more effectively.

In the end, there are methods to undergo a process of relearning attachment, enabling you or your loved one to foster healthier relationships.

CHAPTER ONE

What Is Exactly Fearful Avoidant Attachment

The fearful avoidant attachment style during adulthood corresponds to an insecure attachment style, which is linked to a disorganized attachment style during childhood. Adults with a fearful attachment exhibit both high levels of anxiety and avoidance simultaneously. Despite a strong yearning for closeness, they shy away from intimacy due to negative expectations and a fear of rejection. Additionally, they hold pessimistic views about themselves and others.

The fearful attachment style is commonly associated with experiences of childhood trauma. Among the four attachment styles, individuals with a fearful-avoidant style typically exhibit more unfavorable outcomes.

Signs of fearful avoidant attachment

The signs of a fearful-avoidant attachment can differ among individuals, and both children and adults with this attachment style may exhibit only a subset of the signs provided below. Some individuals may predominantly demonstrate characteristics associated with avoidant attachment, while others may display more signs indicative of fearful attachment.

It's important to note that numerous signs mentioned here could also be symptomatic of underlying mental health conditions such as depression and social anxiety, and may not exclusively signify fearful-avoidant attachment.

The Signs in children

- Expressing internal conflict regarding their desire for closeness with their caregiver.
- Demonstrating distress upon separation from their caregiver, yet exhibiting anger or disinterest upon reunification.
- Displaying challenges in self-regulation, evidenced by frequent temper tantrums or emotional meltdowns.
- Rarely experiencing a sense of safety.

- Exhibiting weak personal boundaries, vacillating between oversharing and withholding information.
- Seeking adult attention but promptly rejecting it once received.
- Struggling to maintain long-term friendships.
- Displaying a lack of differentiation in affection between strangers and loved ones.

Even though they form during early childhood, attachment styles can persist and influence relationships throughout adulthood.

The Signs in adults

- Sharing personal feelings with others is a challenge for you.
- Maintaining conversations at a surface level is preferred as delving into vulnerability feels uncomfortable.
- Both self and others are viewed through a negative lens.
- Establishing meaningful connections seems elusive.

- Swiftly cutting ties with those who cause emotional harm is a common response.
- Frequently disengaging from emotional experiences is a coping mechanism.
- There is a yearning for a profound and loving relationship, accompanied by concerns about the possibility of finding one.
- Sustaining relationships over an extended period poses difficulties.
- Withdrawal is a common response when feeling vulnerable or emotional.
- Finding it challenging to self-soothe during emotional moments.
- Deep-seated beliefs about being let down or hurt by others persist.
- Agreeing to relationships, including intimate ones, may occur even when personal desires are unclear.

Individuals exhibiting a fearful-avoidant attachment style in adulthood may be at a heightened risk for mental health conditions such as depression and social anxiety. Additionally, they might engage in more frequent and varied sexual partnerships.

CHAPTER TWO

What led to the causes fearful avoidant attachment?

While the origins of a fearful-avoidant attachment style may not always be evident, it is frequently linked to the parenting provided by caregivers. Various parenting styles can contribute to the development of a fearful-avoidant attachment, including the following:

1. Trauma or Abuse

Frequently, individuals who have undergone abuse or trauma during their childhoods with caregivers tend to develop a fearful-avoidant attachment style.

In reaction to abuse, a child becomes caught in a cycle between deactivation, as the caregiver cannot provide reassurance, and hyperactivation, as the frightening caregiver consistently triggers attachment needs. The child urgently seeks comfort but has learned that their caregiver is unable to provide it.

2. Broken Trust

From the perspective of a child with a fearful-avoidant attachment, their caregivers are perceived as untrustworthy.

Parenting patterns may exhibit significant inconsistency, transitioning from warmth and affection to coldness and emotional distance abruptly. Such unpredictable parenting makes it challenging for the child to anticipate their parent's reactions, leading to heightened feelings of insecurity.

The parent might frequently make promises to the child but fails to fulfill them, such as committing to perform certain actions, offering support in times of need, or pledging to refrain from yelling. When these assurances go unfulfilled, it further reinforces the child's perception that trusting others is unreliable.

3. Threatening Language

The use of harmful language by a caregiver, involving threats, can undermine a child's sense of security in the relationship. This may encompass employing threats of punishment or physical violence to instill fear in the child. When a child perceives their caregivers as sources of fear, they also learn that having constructive and supportive communication with them is not reliable.

4. Emotionally Needy Caregivers

Parents who rely on their children to fulfill their emotional needs can inadvertently harm their offspring.

These caregivers may express their desires and requirements to their child, at times expecting the child to shoulder this emotional burden or resolve issues independently. When caregivers use the child to meet their own emotional needs, there is a risk of neglecting the child's emotional and physical well-being.

The child will also grasp the notion that their needs are not prioritized as much as those of others. The child might even assume the role of an emotional caretaker for their parent, further intensifying the parent's dependence on the child to fulfill their needs.

5. Caregivers with Fearful-Avoidant Attachment

If a child exhibits a fearful-avoidant attachment style, it is probable that their caregivers also share this attachment style.

This correlation does not imply a genetic influence on attachment styles; instead, it suggests the perpetuation of behavioral patterns across generations. It is likely that a caregiver's own parents contributed to their development of a fearful-avoidant attachment, creating a cycle that continues through subsequent generations.

If the child's insecure attachment is not addressed, they may go on to raise their own children who also develop a fearful-avoidant attachment.

Is it possible for a fearful-avoidant attachment style to undergo changes as time progresses?

Certainly, a fearful-avoidant attachment style has the potential to transform over time through increased self-awareness, personal development, and therapeutic interventions.

Taking steps to address underlying fears and unresolved traumas enables individuals to cultivate more secure attachment patterns.

Establishing positive relationships, honing effective communication skills, and seeking professional assistance are all factors that can contribute to a gradual transition toward a more secure attachment style.

Nevertheless, the speed and degree of this transformation may differ for each individual, influenced by their distinct experiences and commitment to personal development.

CHAPTER THREE

The Impact of Fearful-Avoidant Attachment Style on Your Life

As humans, an innate inclination drives us to pursue companionship, whether in the form of friendships or romantic relationships. The need for others is inherent in our lives. Yet, when a fear of intimacy is present, these conflicting desires can significantly impact your life. However, there are ways to address and overcome this challenge, and we will guide you through the process.

1. Unstable and harmful relationships

The prominent consequence of a fearful-avoidant attachment style is the instability of relationships. Given the simultaneous desire for and fear of intimacy, your connections often become an emotional rollercoaster. Regrettably, studies have indicated that individuals with an anxious-avoidant attachment style are more prone to engaging with violent partners compared to those with other attachment styles.

In this manner, the prediction of experiencing hurt from someone you love becomes a reality. Our subconscious mind has a tendency to manifest our beliefs, making it crucial to seek assistance from someone who comprehends the workings of your subconscious.

2. Casual Sexual Encounters

The fearful-avoidant attachment style can influence one's attitude towards sex. Engaging in casual sex might serve as a means of sidestepping the anxiety associated with long-term relationships for individuals with this attachment style.

This particular attachment style carries the highest psychological and relational risks. Fearfully-avoidant individuals tend to have a greater number of sexual partners and exhibit higher sexual compliance. However, such behavior may lead to significant health issues and social disapproval, impacting self-esteem.

3. Diminished Self-Confidence

Individuals with a fearful-avoidant attachment style often experience low self-confidence, and this comes as no surprise. As mentioned earlier, our lives are influenced by our subconscious beliefs. When you anticipate being hurt and rejected by others, you recognize that such an expectation requires a substantial justification. Your mind has found this justification in the belief that you are not worthy of love.

Undoubtedly, low self-esteem can lead to numerous challenges. As we've discussed, you might seek out toxic, abusive partners who continually reinforce the idea that you are unworthy. This lack of confidence can also impact various aspects of your life, hindering the pursuit of your aspirations and potentially resulting in underperformance academically and professionally.

Ultimately, you may find yourself consistently experiencing emotional turmoil and feeling distressed.

4. Emotional Disruptions

The amalgamation of a pessimistic perception of others (such as "People are hurtful") and oneself ("I am unworthy of kindness") frequently creates a bleak vision of the future. The belief that you are destined to either experience hurt or endure loneliness throughout your life sets the stage for a perfect storm conducive to depressive disorders.

Individuals with a fearful-avoidant attachment style face an elevated risk of developing depression and anxiety. Consequently, the impact of your attachment style may extend beyond romantic relationships, affecting various aspects of your entire life.

How to Overcome Fearful Avoidant Attachment style

If you acquired a fearful-avoidant attachment style in childhood, it could continue to influence your relationships and daily life today, especially if neither you nor your parent sought intervention to address the attachment in your earlier years. Nonetheless, there are still methods to address and overcome a fearful-avoidant attachment style, enabling you to cultivate healthy and loving relationships.

- Enhance your understanding: Familiarize yourself with the fearful-avoidant attachment style and comprehend how it influences your current relationships. Develop an awareness of instances when this attachment style hinders your connections.
- Seek internal validation: Cease the habit of seeking approval and validation from external sources. Discover how to cultivate

self-love from within, reducing dependence on the approval of others.

- Establish personal boundaries: Individuals with a fearful-avoidant attachment style often struggle with setting boundaries, either oversharing or maintaining excessive distance. Identify your boundaries and determine what is necessary for you to feel at ease in relationships.
- Express your needs: Rather than waiting for others to demonstrate affection, communicate your needs to make them aware of what is essential for you to feel valued. For instance, inform your partner if you require more words of affirmation.
- Acquire the crucial skill of self-regulation: In moments of feeling neglected in your relationships, develop the ability to recognize and manage these distressing emotions. Self-soothing is a valuable skill in this context.
- Enhance conflict resolution abilities: Instead of resorting to cutting people out of your life

when tempted, consider giving them a second chance. Employ healthy communication skills to navigate through conflicts, even if it feels uncomfortable, rather than opting for avoidance.
- Explore therapy options: Individuals with this attachment style may struggle with knowing how to navigate emotional situations. A therapist can assist in facilitating challenging conversations, both with oneself and loved ones, regarding emotions and feelings. Through therapy, you can relearn how to respond to one another in a healthy manner.
- Provide reassurance: If your partner or loved one exhibits this attachment style, their underlying fear may involve the concern of abandonment or the desire to leave. Offering comfort and support during this period of self-awareness and transformation can significantly contribute to building confidence.

- Prioritize self-worth: Individuals with insecure attachments frequently grapple with low self-esteem, impacting various relationships. Allow yourself the time and space to recognize which relationships are worth investing in and which may not be. Gradually, you can develop healthier communication patterns, making an intimate, long-term relationship achievable.
- Foster openness: Those with a fearful-avoidant attachment style yearn for intimacy but also harbor significant fear surrounding it. Encourage them to share their feelings and fears, but do so without being forceful. Aggressive approaches may lead them to withdraw.

CONCLUSION

Attachment serves as the foundational means through which humans acquire the ability to interact and communicate with each other.

While some individuals possess robust and healthy attachment styles, others may exhibit less secure patterns, potentially resulting in self-destructive behaviors such as avoiding relationships and fearing intimacy.

The positive news is that you have the capacity to alter your attachment style. While it may necessitate time, effort, and substantial understanding from those in your life, building intimate, secure relationships that bring fulfillment and a sense of safety is entirely achievable.

Made in the USA
Las Vegas, NV
15 March 2025